BREAKING INTO FINANCE MARKET

Insider Strategies For Finding Your Dream Job

PETER ROBBINS

Copyright Page

All rights reserved. No part of this publication may be reproduced, distributed, or transmitted in any form or by any means, including photocopying, recording, or other electronic or mechanical methods, without the prior written permission of the publisher, except in the case of brief quotations embodied in critical reviews and certain other noncommercial uses permitted by copyright law.

Table of Contents

Overview Of Finance Market 4

1: Laying The Foundation... 7

   Understanding the Finance Industry 7

   Essential Skills for Finance Professionals.................... 11

   Building Your Finance Knowledge Base..................... 17

2: Preparing to Break In... 22

   The Job Search Strategies 22

   Creating a Winning Finance Resume and Cover Letter 29

3: Moving Up the Ladder... 33

   Personal Branding in Finance 33

   Handling Rejection and Bouncing Back .... **Error! Bookmark not defined.**

   Actionable Steps To Start Today 40

4: Long-Term Career Success... 48

   Achieving Work-Life Balance in a Demanding Industry 48

   The Future of Finance: Preparing for What's Next....... 54

Overview Of Finance Market

It may be both exhilarating and intimidating to navigate the financial job market, much like jumping into a large ocean. With so many different industries, professions, and career paths, it is critical to comprehend the market to navigate your professional path successfully.

The finance sector, which includes a variety of industries like corporate finance, asset management, investment banking, and financial technology (fintech), is an essential pillar of the world economy. These fields each provide different professional routes, difficulties, and opportunities. For example, investment banking can result in large financial benefits but is linked to high-pressure workplaces and lengthy hours. Conversely, positions in asset management might offer a more balanced lifestyle in addition to high pay.

At the moment, there is a rising need for qualified individuals in the financial industry. Industry sources state that there is a growing demand for finance specialists with the ability to traverse complicated financial environments as countries recover and change after the epidemic. Companies are looking for people who can adapt and flourish in this changing environment for a variety of reasons, including risk management and regulatory compliance. Furthermore, the fintech industry, where innovation is generating new solutions and efficiency, offers great prospects as a result of the development of technology in finance.

However, it is critical to acknowledge that there is intense rivalry. It is important to stand out from the crowd because many professionals and recent grads are fighting for few available employments. Employers value individuals with good interpersonal skills, critical thinking abilities, and technical proficiency in addition to other attributes. This implies that you may greatly improve your prospects by creating a well-rounded profile that highlights both your technical expertise and your soft abilities.

Furthermore, the employment market in finance is always changing. The emergence of big data analytics, blockchain technology, and artificial intelligence is changing and inventing new professions. Professionals who are prepared to adapt to these changes and keep learning new things will be in a better position to take advantage of possibilities as they present themselves.

As you set out on your financial career, keep in mind that learning about the employment market is just the start. This book will walk you through the tactics and insider knowledge required to enter, flourish in, and eventually excel in this fascinating sector. Your ideal financial career is attainable with the correct planning and attitude. Let us examine in more detail what it takes to create a strong basis for your success in the future.

1: Laying The Foundation

Understanding the Finance Industry

When you first walk into the finance industry, it can seem like a big complicated, world but once you break it down, it becomes easier to navigate. The management of money whether, it be through capital-raising investments or just effective money management for people businesses, or governments is the fundamental function of the finance sector. To build a successful career it's important to understand the main areas of finance and what they involve. Essential Financial Sectors.

The finance industry is made up of several key sectors each offering its unique roles and opportunities:

• **Investment banking**: When people hear the word finance, they frequently think of this first. By issuing stocks or bonds and providing merger and acquisition advisory services investment banks assist businesses in raising capital. The work is fast-paced and frequently requires long hours but there are substantial potential benefits in terms of pay and career advancement.

• **Asset Management:** Experts in this field look after client's investments whether they be big organizations like pension funds or private individuals. Investing in stocks bonds real estate and other assets is one way to help clients increase their wealth. Building trust with clients is essential in this field so relationship management and analytical work are combined.

• **Corporate Finance:** In this field, experts work closely with businesses to oversee their financial affairs choose investments, and guarantee the company's viability. This can involve anything from financial planning and budgeting to assessing possible business ventures and confirming that an organization can reach its target profitability.

• **Private equity and venture capital** are two industries that concentrate on making investments in privately held businesses. Private equity involves purchasing shares in well-established companies while venture capital focuses on funding start-ups with significant growth potential. While creating businesses is exciting in these fields there is risk involved because not all investments turn a profit.

- **Fintech:** which stands for financial technology is one of the financial sectors that is expanding the fastest. Here businesses are developing tech-driven solutions for banking lending investing and other financial needs. It's where innovation and finance collide. For those who are interested in technology and finance, this is an exciting field that offers the chance to work in a more flexible and dynamic setting.

Selecting the Correct Course of Action. It's crucial to consider which of the many sectors best suits your interests and skill set. A career in investment banking may be a good fit for you if you enjoy solving complicated problems and perform well under pressure. Finance advisory or asset management positions may be more your style if you're more interested in assisting others in managing their finances and accumulating wealth. Your choice should be based on your objectives and personal strengths. From people who enjoy working with clients and developing relationships to those who prefer a more analytical role the finance industry has something to offer everyone.

The Finance Industry Is Evolving. It's also worth noting that the finance industry is constantly changing. Roles and opportunities are changing due to advancements in technology and changes in global markets. For instance, while fintech is expanding quickly automation is having an impact on traditional finance jobs. In this fast-paced industry, your ability to adapt and be receptive to learning new skills will help you remain relevant.

Finding your place in the industry and being aware of its main sectors are essential to understanding the finance sector. You can more effectively plan your career path after you have a better understanding of the industry. The first step to success is determining which industry best suits your abilities and objectives because each one has its special rewards and difficulties. As you proceed keep in mind that the secret to succeeding in finance will be to keep up with industry trends and to keep learning new things.

Essential Skills for Finance Professionals

Proficiency in finance is imperative across diverse sectors such as accounting banking investment and business management. The ability to budget analyzes finances solve problems evaluate risks plan finances and more are all crucial for the field of finance. Better financial judgment and a deeper comprehension of the economy are the results of these abilities. Employers greatly value finance skills which can lead to career advancement and increased earning potential if you're interested in pursuing a career in finance.

Finance skills are a valuable asset in both personal and professional life and they can be acquired and developed by anyone with the right training and development.

1. interpersonal and communication abilities. For several reasons, communication and interpersonal skills are essential for finance professionals. First and foremost, handling complex financial data that needs to be presented to client's stakeholders or other team members is a requirement for finance professionals. Success in any finance-related career depends on your ability to communicate ideas clearly and succinctly.

Second, you will collaborate closely with clients and coworkers to accomplish common objectives. You can create relationships establish trust and promote productive teamwork with the support of strong interpersonal skills. Finally, it's also important to engage with people from various backgrounds and cultures. You can handle these situations with grace and ease if you have excellent interpersonal and communication skills.

2. Aptitude for Solving Problems. For any career in finance, the ability to solve problems is a must. There are always going to be obstacles in this field from intricate financial computations to strategic choices that have a big effect on a business's bottom line. You can take on these problems head-on analyze data and come up with original solutions if you have strong problem-solving abilities. Additionally, by using these abilities you can spot possible issues before they happen and take proactive measures to avoid them. Critical thinking meticulousness and a willingness to collaborate with others to accomplish common objectives are necessary for effective problem-solving in the finance industry.

3 Morals and Ethics: Any finance professional must have strong ethical principles because managing other people's money and choosing investments call for a great deal of accountability. It is imperative that you identify and steer clear of conflicts of interest safeguard sensitive data and make financially and morally sound choices. Adherence to stringent ethical standards and codes of conduct is mandatory for regulatory bodies and financial institutions with severe penalties for noncompliance. As a result, finance professionals need to have strong ethical principles.

4. Accounting Abilities. Accurate and efficient financial data analysis is made possible by accounting. Comprehending accounting concepts aids in assessing the financial performance of an organization recognizing patterns projecting future results making financial plans controlling risks and guaranteeing regulatory compliance. To summarize accounting knowledge is required. Monetary disclosure. Financial evaluation. Setting a budget. Making plans. Observance. Control of risks.

5. Strategic Abilities in Financial Planning: financial-strategic planning. Financial planning is an essential component of the financial world and is vital to accomplishing a company's goals so if you haven't already you should devote time and energy to honing your skills in this area. Financial planning is becoming more and more crucial for businesses as they deal with financial difficulties because it helps them avoid financial pitfalls and establish a plan for future stability. Making wise decisions and efficiently allocating resources to meet company objectives is made possible by having a solid understanding of financial planning. It also enables the identification of possible financial risks and opportunities as well as the development of plans to reduce or take advantage of them.

6. Proficiency in financial reporting: The ability to assess a company's financial performance and health makes financial reporting essential. To make wise investment decisions financial reports offer crucial details about a company's income costs profits and cash flow. A solid understanding of accounting principles and financial statements such as balance sheets income statements and cash flow statements is necessary to improve financial reporting abilities. Comprehending and evaluating financial data also necessitates an understanding of financial analysis methods and instruments like trend and ratio analysis.

7. Analytical Abilities: Due to their exposure to complex financial models and vast amounts of data finance professionals greatly value their analytical abilities. Finance professionals can recognize trends evaluate and analyze financial data and make defensible decisions thanks to these abilities. Making well-informed decisions that assist organizations in reaching their financial objectives can be facilitated by having a solid grasp of analytical skills which can help you spot trends risks and opportunities in financial data.

8. Skills in Project Management: Because it entails planning and budgeting analyzing financial data and making defensible decisions regarding resource allocation project management is an essential finance skill. The timely cost-effective and high-quality completion of projects by finance professionals can lead to improved financial performance in the long run. This is made possible by effective project management.

9. Digital Tool Proficiency: It's no secret that today's best jobs require a high level of computer proficiency. Any career in finance operates similarly. Being proficient in multiple software programs is essential as the majority of financial documentation needs to be completed via computers. You suggest that you have extensive knowledge of financial data organization in a digital format by putting digital tools on your resume. You should be familiar with the following digital tools among others.

10. Both Qualitative and Quantitative Methods for Risk Analysis: To assess possible risks in financial decisions a finance professional needs to possess both quantitative and qualitative risk analysis skills. You can guarantee the long-term success of financial institutions and investments by using these skills to identify and prioritize major risks and develop strategies to mitigate or avoid them. Whereas qualitative analysis uses expert judgment and subjective assessment for risks that are difficult to quantify quantitative analysis uses mathematical and statistical models to estimate risk probability and impact.

Building Your Finance Knowledge Base

It is crucial to have a strong knowledge base before attempting to enter the finance sector. Employers in the technical field of finance expect you to possess a solid understanding of important concepts tools and trends. But don't worry you won't have to become an expert at this right away. It's all about gradually building your knowledge and continuously learning as you grow in your career.

Now let's explore some methods for beginning to expand your knowledge base in finance.

Consider starting with the fundamentals. The first thing to do if you're new to finance is to familiarize yourself with the fundamental ideas that guide the sector. Any position in finance requires an understanding of basic terms like cash flow income statements balance sheets and return on investment (ROI). Fortunately, there are a ton of easily accessible online resources for beginners ranging from free finance courses to YouTube tutorials that clearly and concisely explain these ideas. Study financial markets (such as stocks bonds and commodities) interest rates and the functioning of the economy in addition to financial statements. Your understanding of these subjects will improve your ability to see how finance fits into the overall structure of international markets.

Print and Digital Materials: Reading books on finance is a great way to increase your knowledge. Classics like The Intelligent Investor by Benjamin Graham or Principles by Ray Dalio are fantastic starting points because they explain investment strategies and financial principles straightforwardly. Books like Simon Benningas's Financial Modeling provide a practical understanding of the technical skills required in the field for more hands-on learning. You also have access to an abundance of online resources. Websites like Investopedia break down finance terms and concepts in simple language making it easier to understand even the more complex aspects of the industry. Additionally, platforms such as Coursera Udemy and LinkedIn Learning provide courses frequently taught by subject matter experts on a variety of topics from basic accounting to advanced financial analysis. Follow Industry

News Up to Date: Being current with current events is crucial because the finance industry is always changing. The

Wall Street Journal Financial Times and Bloomberg are excellent resources for learning about the most recent trends shifts in the market and modifications to regulations in the financial sector. You can stay informed about pertinent topics even by subscribing to finance-related accounts on social media or podcasts. By reading up on industry news you'll not only build your knowledge but also gain insight into how external factors such as government policies and global events impact financial markets. This helps you develop a more nuanced understanding of the industry and shows potential employers that you're serious about your career.

Realistic Skills are Important: Finance is a practical field that goes beyond theory so having these skills will help you stand out. Excel is one of the most useful tools in finance. Excel is essential for budgeting data analysis and financial modeling. Excel is taught in a plethora of online tutorials and courses designed specifically for finance professionals. Learning how to use pivot tables VLOOKUP and financial formulas like internal rate of return (IRR) and net present value (NPV) will be important. Learn how to analyze data using financial modeling software or programming languages like Python if you're going for a more quantitative career. Particularly in fields like fintech or investment banking these abilities can make you stand out in the competitive job market.

Examine Certifications: Getting certified is an additional means of enhancing your credibility and understanding of finance. Because they offer in-depth study of financial subjects' programs such as the Chartered Financial Analyst (CFA) or Certified Public Accountant (CPA) are highly regarded in the business. Even though obtaining these certifications takes effort and time they can greatly improve your resume and lead to more senior positions. If you're just getting started you might think about getting certified as a Financial Risk Manager (FRM) or Financial Modeling and Valuation Analyst (FMVA) which are less time-consuming but still useful certifications.

Discover via Action: Applying what you've learned is one of the finest ways to expand your knowledge base in finance. It's not necessary to work in finance to begin practicing. You can start a blog where you analyze financial trends make a mock portfolio or track your investments. You'll get more at ease with the concepts the more you work with actual finance problems. Additional sources of useful experience include volunteer work side projects and internships. You can gain practical experience and develop skills that you can demonstrate to potential employers by working on a small-scale project such as aiding a local business with their finances or helping with investment analysis.

Although it takes time expanding your knowledge in finance is essential to securing your ideal position in the field. Start with the fundamentals delve into pertinent literature and online courses and keep up with news from the industry. Concentrate on honing in-demand practical skills such as Excel and financial modeling and think about getting certified to expand your knowledge. Above all don't hesitate to put what you've learned into practice. Your confidence and readiness for success in the finance industry will both increase as your knowledge base expands.

2: Preparing to Break In

The Job Search Strategies

Knowing the current trends in the market is the first step toward conducting a successful job search. Industries are always changing certain sectors grow quickly while others encounter difficulties. It's critical to determine which fields are in demand and to match your professional objectives with these fields. It's possible to discover new opportunities by staying up to date with emerging technologies and industries according to resources such as the Institute for Employment Studies (IES).

1. Writing a Standout Cover Letter. Your resume is often your first impression with potential employers. It should be unique to each job application highlighting accomplishments and relevant skills. Put your attention on particular experiences and abilities that relate to the position you're applying for. You can make sure your resume is organized and professional by using resume-building websites and online templates. Keep in mind that having a strong CV can greatly increase your chances of getting an interview.

2. Making Your LinkedIn Profile Shine. An elegant LinkedIn profile is crucial in the current digital era. Include a full work history and a professional photo in your updated profile. Your job search can be greatly aided by using LinkedIn to build your network and interact with industry-related content. You can locate positions that fit your interests and skill set with the LinkedIn job search function. You can also keep up to date on the newest job openings and industry trends by joining LinkedIn groups that are relevant to your line of work.

3. Cover Letter Art. A strong cover letter can make a big difference in your job application. For every application, it should be unique and clearly state why you are the best person for the job. Put your best qualities and experiences which your resume does not address that are pertinent to the position to the front of the cover letter. Your ability to communicate effectively and your excitement for the job can be seen in an effective cover letter which will set you apart from the competition.

4. Smart Networking. A crucial aspect of job searching is networking. Do not hesitate to request informational interviews and attend career fairs and industry events. Creating connections may open doors to untapped employment opportunities. Connecting with peers and leaders in the industry is facilitated by professional networking sites and online networks. In addition to providing you with information about various companies and career paths, networking can help you focus and expedite your job search.

5. Interview Readying. Interview preparation is very important. Do your homework on the business and the position rehearse standard interview questions and make sure you project a professional and assured image. Typical interview questions and suggested responses can be found online. You can also hone your answers and boost your confidence by doing practice interviews with friends or mentors. Recall that being well-prepared can have a big impact on how well you perform in the real interview.

6. Using Search Engines for Jobs. You can use job search engines by creating job alerts and by using keywords that are specific to the position you want. Finding appropriate job openings can be greatly increased by doing this. You can use the advanced search features on websites such as Indeed Glassdoor and LinkedIn to filter jobs according to industry region and job type. With the aid of these features, you can focus your search and identify the best job openings that fit your preferences and skill set.

7. Managing Opportunities for Remote Work. Your applications highlight abilities like communication self-control and time management given the popularity of remote work. Orienting your job search toward organizations that provide remote work opportunities may prove advantageous. Flexible work roles can be found with the aid of job search websites that specialize in remote work opportunities. Highlighting your ability to work independently and manage your time effectively can make you an attractive candidate for remote jobs.

8. Ongoing Professional Growth. Continuous learning and skill development are critical in a job market that is always changing. Participating in workshops and courses helps you stay competitive and flexible. Online learning environments provide new certifications and abilities that apply to your line of work. You can stay ahead of the curve in the job market and discover new career opportunities by keeping up with industry trends and consistently honing your skills.

9. Making the Most of Internet Resources for Job Search. You can improve your chances of landing the ideal job by using a variety of job search engines. Job listings that are not available on other websites can be found with the help of distinctive features found on websites such as Indeed Glassdoor Monster LinkedIn and so forth. By creating job alerts saving job searches and applying to jobs directly through the website users can make the most of these platforms. Your job search net will become wider the more platforms you use which will increase the likelihood that you will find the best opportunities.

10. Customizing Your Employment Seek. Search for a job by focusing on the industry and your own career goals. Make use of industry-specific keywords in your cover letter online profiles and resume. When employers utilize applicant tracking systems (ATS) to screen applicants this can make your applications stand out. You can save time and improve your chances of success by narrowing down your job search to particular industries and roles.

11. Professional Associations Role. Acquiring membership in professional associations associated with your area of expertise can offer beneficial networking prospects and tools for your employment pursuits. Numerous associations provide networking opportunities career guidance and job boards to help you connect with employers and grow your career. You can stay up to date on job opportunities and industry trends by using the resources offered by these associations. A proactive and flexible strategy will be necessary in the job market of 2024 and beyond. Through the strategic use of technology efficient networking and ongoing skill development, you set yourself up for success in this ever-changing job market. The greatest opportunities can be located with the aid of job search engines and online job search platforms. Make sure your CV and LinkedIn profile are up to date and focus your job search on positions that align with your professional objectives. Recall that overcoming the challenges of the modern job market requires tenacity and flexibility. Utilizing all of the resources at your disposal and always enhancing your abilities will help you stay competitive and accomplish your professional objectives. You can successfully navigate online platforms and find hidden opportunities by using these strategies in your job search which will ultimately lead to a successful career in your chosen field.

12. Gaining an awareness of the company culture. It's important to know the company culture when applying for jobs. Investigating the business can help you ascertain whether it is in line with your professional objectives by providing you with information about its values and workplace culture. To gain an idea of what it's like to work at the company read reviews and articles.

13. Interacting with Company Overviews. A lot of businesses keep their LinkedIn and other social media accounts updated. You can keep up with the most recent information and job opportunities on these profiles by liking commenting and sharing their content. This interaction demonstrates your interest in the business and may increase your appeal as a candidate.

14. Understanding the Hiring Process. Hiring procedures vary amongst businesses. While certain may require practical tests or assessments others may consist of multiple interview rounds. You may improve your chances of success and prepare more effectively by being aware of the hiring procedure used by the company you are applying to. You can get a better idea of what to expect by reading about other people's experiences who have gone through the hiring process at the company.

Creating a Winning Finance Resume and Cover Letter

A finance cover letter needs to be many things at once: professional succinct and appealing to the employer or recruiter. The success of your cover letter depends on its hook which should provide background information supporting details and your motivation for the position. When you submit your cover letter in finance or accounting you have the opportunity to elaborate on how your experience has equipped you for your next professional step beyond what is listed on your resume.

1. Strike a balance between form and function. Provide a clear and concise cover letter that highlights your qualifications for the position who you are and what you are looking for. When composing your cover piece ensure that it is formatted like a letter with your contact information an appropriate salutation (including the name of the recruiter or interviewer) and a closing statement such as 'yours sincerely'. Depending on the kind of role we advise composing three to four customized paragraphs (of roughly 300 to 400 words each) which should include an introduction a justification for your interest in the job and a mention of how you learned about it.

2. Offer Proof. Your cover letter's first two to three paragraphs should explain why you are interested in the position why you would like to work for the company and why they should hire you for a position such as financial controller accountant or director of finance. The employer is evaluating whether you will be a valuable addition to the accounting firm or organization as well as your ability to perform the job at hand with a foundation of skills experience and expertise.

Giving measurable examples of past successes is the most effective way to achieve these objectives.

• As opposed to stating I used financial modeling and forecasting skills to make strategic business recommendations in my previous role as financial controller at a global manufacturing firm.

• You could write I used financial modeling and forecasting skills to analyze market trends in my previous role as financial controller at a global manufacturing firm resulting in a 15% increase in revenue projections for the upcoming fiscal year. This provided valuable information for strategic business recommendations that helped launch a successful product surpass sales goals by 20% and increase overall profitability.

3 Key words and qualifications. The employer will find your cover letter more compelling if it highlights your qualifications for the job including any specialized training certifications and relevant education. Make sure you have the necessary skills and experience for the position by using relevant keywords from the job description.

4. Display Your Knowledge of the Company and Modify Your Tone. You have to do your homework on the business or accounting firm you are applying to before you write your cover letter. When describing how your abilities meet the needs of the company and how you can help it succeed it is helpful to show that you have done your homework on the organization and are aware of its values culture goals and standing in the industry. Your application should always be professional regardless of whether the company uses a business-like tone of voice on its website newsletters and messaging or culture-centric casual messaging behind its brand.

5. Adjust Handle Issues and Give Thanks. It should go without saying that you should tailor your cover letter to each job application. Sending a generic letter won't get you to the interview stage. Highlight specific elements of your background that are pertinent to the position and organization show that you are excited about the work and don't forget to mention any gaps in your employment history or the reasons behind your decision to change careers if you're changing paths. It's a good idea to end your cover letter by thanking the employer for the opportunity to apply and restating your interest in the business. Don't forget to include a call to action like indicating that you are available for additional discussion or that you hope to be interviewed.

3: Moving Up the Ladder

Personal Branding in Finance

Finance Personal Branding. Particularly in the finance industry, your brand is just as crucial in today's cutthroat job market as your technical skills and qualifications. The goal of personal branding is to establish your professional identity highlight your advantages and differentiate yourself in a crowded market. Building a strong personal brand can attract opportunities open doors and accelerate career growth in the finance industry where expertise trust and credibility are critical.

Here's how to grow and use your brand in the financial industry.

Define Personal Branding. Fundamentally personal branding is how you show yourself to the outside world your distinct set of abilities life experiences moral principles and distinctive personality that sets you apart. As a finance professional, it's the narrative you present about yourself. You have a personal brand already whether you know it or not. People think of your reputation when they hear your name. Your brand affects how people see you including client's colleagues and potential employers in the finance industry where relationships and trust are crucial. Having a strong brand makes you more visible and credible and demonstrates your expertise and dependability in your industry.

The Significance of Personal Branding in Finance

1. Differentiation within a Competitive Industry. Talented professionals with similar backgrounds experiences and technical skills abound in the finance industry. Your brand is what distinguishes you from someone else who has the same degree or certifications. Whether it's your capacity for critical thought under duress your talent for demystifying intricate financial ideas to clients or your proficiency in a particular field like risk management or fintech it draws attention to your special value. When applying for jobs attending networking events or making client pitches having a clear and distinct brand helps you stand out and become memorable.

2. Establishing Credibility and Trust. The foundation of finance is trust. People must have faith in you when you manage investments handle confidential financial information or counsel clients on important financial decisions. You can demonstrate your honesty competence and professionalism through your brand all of which are critical for establishing and preserving that trust. Through your work online presence and interactions with clients and colleagues you establish yourself as a reliable and trustworthy professional by continuously showcasing your knowledge and values.

3. Call for Opportunities. Opportunities such as partnerships speaking engagements job offers and promotions can be drawn in by having a strong personal brand. As you build your reputation and expertise in a particular area people will start to recognize you as a go-to person for that niche. For example, if you brand yourself as an expert in sustainable finance or cryptocurrency, you're more likely to be approached for roles or projects that align with that expertise.

How to Establish Your Brand in the Finance Industry.

1. Discover Your Particular Advantages. Finding your unique selling point is the first step in creating your brand. What are your main advantages over others? What knowledge or abilities make you stand out from the crowd? Perhaps you're an excellent communicator or have a keen analytical mind. Alternatively, you might be passionate about fintech and keep up with all the latest developments in that field. Consider the attributes that people find admirable in you such as your technical proficiency capacity for leadership or even soft skills like teamwork and communication. Your brand is constructed from these foundational elements.

2. Identify Your Specialty. Since the finance sector is so large it's helpful to identify your niche. Which aspect of finance most excites you? It could be personal financial planning corporate finance asset management investment banking or fintech. By concentrating on a particular niche, you establish yourself as an authority in that field which can increase brand recognition and attract the right customers. Building a brand around sustainable finance or ESG

(Environmental Social and Governance) investing for instance could be your priority if you have a strong commitment to environmental sustainability. Possessing a solid reputation as an authority in your field can be quite advantageous.

3. Establish a Web Presence. Your brand is greatly influenced by your online presence in the modern digital world. This is particularly true in the finance industry as prospective peers' clients and employers frequently look you up online before meeting you in person.

Your brand can be greatly improved by having a carefully chosen online presence.

LinkedIn: Make your LinkedIn profile as effective as possible first. It's frequently where people go to find out more information about you initially. A professional photo an attention-grabbing headline that highlights your experience and expertise and a thorough synopsis that highlights your abilities are all necessary for a complete profile. Regularly share articles insights or thoughts on financial trends to show your engagement with the industry.

Personal Website or Blog: To make it happen think about starting a personal website or blog where you can share your knowledge. Composing articles on financial subjects not only establishes you as an authority but also shows your love and dedication to the field.

Social Media: Depending on your niche Twitter or Instagram can be helpful social media platforms but LinkedIn is the main one for finance professionals. Expanding your audience can be achieved by disseminating industry news providing financial advice or participating in conversations regarding the direction of finance.

4. Act with Honesty and Consistency. In terms of personal branding consistency is crucial. Your brand should always represent your personality knowledge and values whether you're communicating online or in person. For instance, if you have a reputation for being analytical and detail-oriented make sure that shows in your work online persona and even in your interactions. Authenticity is also very important. When someone is making an excessive effort to fit a particular image people can tell. Instead of focusing on what you believe you should be your brand should represent who you are as a financial expert. Real connections and trust are essential in finance and authenticity fosters these.

5. Connect and Form Partnerships. The connections you make and the impressions you make on other people are what shape your brand it doesn't exist in a vacuum. For you to develop your brand networking is essential. Engage in online finance communities go to industry events and make connections with people whose work you like. Your credibility as a competent trustworthy and personable financial expert will increase as you cultivate connections and add value to others.

In the finance industry personal branding is more than just promoting yourself it's also about identifying your value and convincingly displaying it to others. You can establish a brand that distinguishes you in the crowded finance sector by focusing on your strengths creating a website strategically networking and building an online presence. In the end, having a strong personal brand will help you build credibility draw in new business, and progress your financial career.

Actionable Steps To Start Today

Take able Actions to Enter the Finance Job Market Right Now. Although it may seem impossible to break into the finance industry the good news is that there are practical doable steps you can take right now to set yourself up for success. Making little calculated moves can help you get closer to securing your ideal finance position regardless of where you are in your career or if you are switching from another industry. Let us now discuss some doable steps that you can take right now.

1. Examine and Determine Which Roles to Aim for. Numerous career paths are available in the broad finance industry including investment banking corporate finance asset management fintech risk management and more. Start by investigating various positions and sectors in the finance industry to see what most interests you if you're not sure where to begin. Begin by asking yourself: Which aspects of finance interest you? Which kind of work do you like better analyzing data dealing with numbers or dealing directly with clients? Which kind of atmosphere would you prefer one that is fast-paced high-pressure or more regimented and predictable? Examine the job descriptions and prerequisites for the roles that interest you after you've determined which ones. This will make it easier for you to comprehend the abilities credentials and work history that you should prioritize.

2. Enhance Your Understanding of Finances. It is still possible to begin expanding your knowledge base in finance even if you do not have a formal background. Being up to date on the newest innovations rules and trends in the finance industry is essential to being a competitive applicant. As an alternative you can: Get financial news by subscribing to publications such as The Wall Street Journal Financial Times Bloomberg or CNBC. Read Financial News Daily. This will assist you in staying informed about company performance market trends and significant industry events.

3. Follow Influential Finance Experts: Follow finance professionals on LinkedIn Twitter or even YouTube channels that focus on financial education. Those who have already made a name for themselves in the field can teach you a lot. Take Advantage of Free Finance Courses: Websites such as Coursera edX and Khan Academy provide inexpensive or free courses on finance-related subjects. To gain a foundational understanding of finance look for courses on financial modeling investment analysis or personal finance.

4. One More Network One More Network. In the financial sector in particular networking is a very effective tool. Getting your foot in the door in the finance industry requires establishing connections with people who are already employed there as most job openings are filled through internal networks or referrals. Participate in Industry Events: Attend webinars seminars or conferences many of which are webcasts. Both learning and networking in the field are greatly facilitated by these events. Use LinkedIn to your advantage: Begin by making connections with finance professionals who hold positions that interest you. Interact with their content leave comments on posts and send them articles or industry-related insights. By doing this you may stand out and establish valuable relationships. Join Financial Communities: Search Reddit Facebook LinkedIn or other social media platforms for communities or groups focused on finance. You can obtain job postings and networking opportunities by joining these groups and gaining insights into the industry. Arrange Informational Interviews: Make contact with experts in finance and request informational interviews. Asking them questions about their career path industry challenges and advice for someone just starting is a laid-back non-job-seeking conversation. It's a great way to establish rapport because people are usually happy to share their experiences.

5. Make Sure Your LinkedIn Profile And Resume Are Up To Date. A strong CV and LinkedIn profile are essential if you're serious about entering the finance industry. Even if they don't directly relate to finance make sure they accurately represent your relevant experiences and skills. Emphasize Transferable Skills: If you don't have any prior experience in finance concentrate on developing your transferable skills. Data analysis problem-solving communication meticulousness and Excel proficiency are all useful in the finance industry. Create a Resume That Is Particular to Each Job: For every finance position you apply for make sure your resume is specific to the job description. Highlight any coursework projects or internships you've done that are related to finance and use keywords from the job posting. Enhance Your LinkedIn Profile: Ensure that your summary and headline effectively express your interest in finance. This is the place to discuss your interest in finance your relevant experience and your ideal position. Make sure your profile is searchable by using finance-related keywords on LinkedIn as recruiters frequently use this platform to find candidates.

6. Practice Interviewing for Jobs in Finance. Job interviews in finance can be quite tough, particularly in industries with high levels of competition like investment banking and private equity. Now is the time to start getting ready for these interviews so you'll be ready when the chance comes up. Learn Frequently Asked Questions for Finance Interviews: Become acquainted with the frequently asked questions for finance interviews including those about financial modeling market trends and problem-solving situations. Practice Behavioral Questions: Behavioral questions are frequently used in finance interviews to determine how well an applicant can tackle challenges collaborate with others and handle pressure. Get comfortable responding to inquiries such as Describe a situation in which you had to solve a complicated problem and How do you handle short deadlines? Technical Skills: You might be questioned on financial statements Excel-based tasks and valuation techniques in positions like investment banking or asset management. Start reviewing financial statements and studying valuation methods such as DCF (Discounted Cash Flow) or comparable company analysis to refresh your memory on these concepts.

7. Apply for Entry-Level Jobs or Internships. An internship or entry-level position can serve as the ideal stepping stone for someone just starting in the finance industry. Through internships, you can expand your network obtain practical experience, and improve the competitiveness of your resume for future employment. Apply for Financial Internships: A lot of financial companies provide internship opportunities, particularly for recent graduates or students. Even if the internship isn't in your ideal position it can still help you network and expose you to the industry. If internships are not an option consider applying for entry-level positions such as associate in operations junior accountant or financial analyst. These jobs can help you establish a solid foundation and acquire the abilities you'll need to progress in your financial career.

8. Continue applying and remaining persistent. Rejection is a common occurrence in the finance industry and breaking in takes time. Before securing the ideal position, you might have to apply to multiple jobs. The important thing is to persevere and not let failures demoralize you.

Apply to a Variety of Jobs: Don't restrict yourself to positions in the finance industry. To improve your chances of discovering a suitable fit apply to several jobs.

Continue Developing Your Skills: Take advantage of any downtime in between applications to continue developing your technical skills growing your network or refining your understanding of finance.

Be Positive: Although there is competition in the finance industry you can find a position that fits your goals if you are persistent well-prepared and take the appropriate approach.

If you want to advance in the finance job market you must act today. Establish your objectives increase your understanding of finance and widen your network first. You can position yourself to stand out and land the finance job you've been dreaming of with patience perseverance and time. Don't wait to get started even tiny actions can have a significant impact. You'll have a better chance of obtaining your ideal finance position the more proactive you are!

4: Long-Term Career Success

Achieving Work-Life Balance in a Demanding Industry

Finding a Work-Life Balance in a Demanding Field. Working in finance frequently entails long hours intense pressure and short turnaround times. The corporate finance asset management and investment banking sectors are all renowned for having fast-paced work environments. Juggling obligations all the time can make it seem impossible to achieve a healthy work-life balance. But it's not only feasible it's essential to your long-term prosperity and welfare. Let's examine doable tactics for surviving in the competitive world of finance and preserving a work-life balance.

1. **Establish Clear and Early Boundaries.** Achieving a work-life balance requires you to draw clear boundaries between your personal and professional spheres. It's simple to let work consume your weekends and evenings when working in the finance industry but burnout is unavoidable if you don't set boundaries.

Action - Let your manager and team know when you're free. For instance, inform them that after a specific hour of the evening, you won't be checking emails unless it's urgent. So that you and your coworkers are aware of when you're off the clock it's critical to set these expectations early on.

Action - Consistently respect your boundaries. Others will not respect your boundaries if you don't. Over time people will adjust to your limits.

2. Set Priorities for Your Work and Time. It's common to feel that everything is urgent in a fast-paced setting. Work smarter not harder by developing your ability to prioritize tasks.

Action: Prioritize your most crucial tasks each morning. Prioritize finishing these before moving on to less important tasks. You can make sure that your energy is focused on the things that matter by doing this.

Action: Organize your time effectively by using tools like productivity apps or time-blocking. To prevent burnout, divide your work into concentrated periods and intersperse them with brief breaks.

3. Acquire the Ability to Politely Say No. It can seem like you have to say yes to every task or project in the finance industry, especially at the beginning of your career. Being proactive is vital but taking on too much at once can easily result in overload.

Action: Don't be hesitant to clarify priorities when you're asked to take on more than you can manage. Say I'd be happy to take that on as an example. But right now, I'm focusing on X. You can control your workload without explicitly declining by asking Would you like me to prioritize this new task over it?

Action: If it's hard for you to say no try assigning yourself small chores when you can or asking for assistance when you need it. It's not necessary for you to bear the whole weight alone.

4. Make Time for Yourself Every Day. Taking care of yourself daily is crucial for preserving your physical and mental well-being regardless of how demanding your work may be. Even if it's only for 15 to 30 minutes made me-time a part of your daily routine. Make the most of this time by engaging in a relaxing or rejuvenating activity such as reading taking a stroll or practicing meditation. Taking care of yourself makes it easier for you to face challenges at work with a clear head.

Action: Look for things to do that make you happy or give you a sense of accomplishment away from work. Engaging in hobbies working out or socializing with loved ones can assist you in unwinding and keeping your equilibrium.

5. Work Smarter by Utilizing Technology. When it comes to work-life balance technology can be both a help and a hindrance. Working from any location is made possible by it but unplugging can be challenging at times. Utilizing technology to your advantage is crucial.

Action: Automate tedious chores or improve your workflow with apps or tools. Time saved for more purposeful work or private pursuits is the result of this.

Action: Use technology to establish boundaries. To prevent continuous distractions, you could for instance turn off work notifications after hours or use Do Not Disturb mode during your time.

6. Take Time Off and Breaks. It might sound counterintuitive but taking breaks and using your vacation time is critical to maintaining work-life balance. Continuously pushing yourself without taking breaks results in reduced productivity job satisfaction and burnout.

Action: If you work long hours, especially during the workday develop the habit of taking brief breaks. You can rejuvenate yourself with even a five-minute walk away from your desk.

Action: Make the most of your vacation days by using them! By taking time off you can recuperate and return to work with fresh vigor and concentration. Plan your vacation during slower times or get in touch with your team to make sure everything goes smoothly if you're afraid of missing out or falling behind.

7. Treat Yourself with Kindness. It takes time to achieve work-life balance it is not something that can be done quickly. There will be days when everything seems under control and days when it feels more overwhelming. It's important to be kind to yourself during the process.

Action: Aim for progress rather than perfection. Acknowledge that you're trying your hardest and when things don't go according to plan try not to be too hard on yourself. Let it go and start over the next day if you've had a difficult day.

Action: Appreciate little victories. Whether it's finishing a project on time or managing to leave the office early acknowledge the progress you're making towards achieving balance.

It's difficult but not impossible to juggle a demanding finance career with a personal life. You can make your career a priority without sacrificing your well-being by establishing boundaries practicing effective time management and prioritizing self-care. Recall that success depends not only on your level of effort but also on how well you look after yourself during the process. A healthier happier life and a sustainable career are the long-term benefits of finding balance even though it may take some time to achieve.

Preparing for What's Next

Being ahead of the curve is crucial for long-term success in the finance industry which is a field that is always changing. The finance landscape of the future will be significantly different from the past due to changes in market dynamics and technology advancements. However, the opportunity also comes with change. You can set yourself up for success in this constantly shifting environment by planning for what's coming up next. Let us examine some of the major themes that will influence the finance industry going forward and what you can do now to get ready for the journey.

1. Digital Innovation and FinTech Ascent. The finance sector is rapidly changing due to technology. Fintech enterprises are causing a stir in the banking industry by providing cutting-edge solutions such as blockchain-based services robot-advisors and digital payments. The need for tech-savvy financial professionals is therefore rising.

Action: Become knowledgeable about fintech tools and trends. Even if technology isn't directly related to your job knowing how fintech is changing the market will increase your adaptability and value to employers. Learn about cryptocurrencies blockchain technology and artificial intelligence applications in finance.

Action: Investigate online courses covering financial technology Python or SQL programming and data analytics. In the digital age having technical skills in your toolbox will help you remain competitive.

2. ESG Investing and Sustainability. Investment decisions are becoming more and more influenced by environmental social and governance (ESG) factors. Businesses that emphasize social responsibility ethics and sustainability are getting more weight from investors. The need for finance experts who comprehend ESG standards and can apply them to financial analysis and investment strategies is increasing as a result of this change.

Action: Keep up with the latest developments in sustainable finance. Examine how corporate policies regulatory changes and investment decisions are impacted by ESG considerations. This information will be crucial as long as investors and businesses prioritize sustainable business practices.

Action- Take into consideration earning certifications or enrolling in classes related to corporate social responsibility (CSR) sustainable finance or ESG investing. Gaining knowledge in this field will help you stand out as a progressive practitioner in the changing world of finance.

3. Developing markets and globalization. While globalization has been a key trend for years the continued growth of emerging markets offers exciting opportunities for finance professionals. Rapid economic development is transforming Latin American Asian and African nations into major players in world finance.

Action - Learn more about international markets and economies especially those in developing nations. Keep abreast of trade regulations market prospects and economic developments in these domains.

Action: If at all possible, learn a new language or hone your cross-cultural communication skills to improve your capacity to collaborate with clients or businesses around the world. As the world's financial systems grow increasingly interwoven this may offer you a competitive advantage.

4. Artificial Intelligence (AI) and Automation. From providing predictive analytics to automating repetitive tasks artificial intelligence and automation are completely changing the way financial institutions operate. Technology improves productivity but it also alters the nature of work in finance. Finance professionals must adjust as AI-powered tools take the place of manual tasks in roles like data entry and basic analysis.

Action: Acknowledge the automation trend by becoming knowledgeable about the use of AI in finance. Recognize its applications in risk management algorithmic trading and fraud detection. Your future readiness will increase with your level of technological understanding.

Action: Put your attention on honing soft skills like problem-solving critical thinking and interpersonal communication as these are less likely to be automated. Even though technology is capable of doing many things creativity and human judgment will always be valued.

5. Regulatory Shifts and Compliance. The financial sector is subject to strict regulations which are updated in tandem with the introduction of new investment products and technologies. For both individuals and institutions adhering to evolving laws and regulations is essential. More regulatory changes are likely in the upcoming years as governments react to trends like fintech cryptocurrencies and ESG investing.

Action - Stay up to date on any changes to regulations that may affect your particular field of finance. Keeping up to date will help you navigate these changes and ensure compliance whether it's new tax laws anti-money laundering (AML) regulations or data privacy laws.

Action: Pursuing certifications such as the Certified Regulatory Compliance Manager (CRCM) or equivalent credentials can help you focus on compliance or risk management. As the regulatory environment changes having expertise in this field will become more and more valuable.

6. The Human Factor: Soft Skills Are More Important Than Ever. Soft skills like communication adaptability and leadership are crucial even though technology and data are largely responsible for the changes in the finance industry. The ability to lead teams manage relationships and make strategic decisions will become increasingly important for top professionals as automation replaces routine tasks.

Action: Prioritize enhancing your soft skills in addition to your technical ones. The finance industry is set to undergo significant globalization and evolution making strong communication emotional intelligence and teamwork skills essential.

Action: Look for chances to lead even if they are modest like managing a project or coaching a coworker. Your career will be more prepared for roles in the more complex tech-driven finance industry if you gain leadership experience early on.

7. We cannot compromise on lifelong learning. Dedicated to lifelong learning is arguably the most crucial component of getting ready for the future of finance. People who take their success for granted run the risk of falling behind as the industry changes more quickly than ever. Long-term success will depend heavily on one's capacity for learning and adapting whether that be through mastering new technologies comprehending developing markets or keeping abreast of regulatory changes.

Action: Schedule frequent professional development sessions to prioritize lifelong learning. Being informed and inquisitive will help you stay ahead of the curve whether you choose to learn through formal courses industry publications or webinars.

Action: Seek out mentors who can offer insights into industry trends attend conferences and become a member of professional associations. You can stay informed about the latest developments in finance by surrounding yourself with knowledgeable people.

Finance has a bright future ahead of it full of challenges and exciting opportunities. The industry is changing as a result of globalization technology sustainability and regulations but those who adapt to these changes and keep up with their skills will be well-positioned. In an ever-changing financial landscape, you can prosper by remaining knowledgeable flexible, and dedicated to lifelong learning. Recall that the financial sector will always require individuals with strategic thinking problem-solving abilities and the ability to form deep connections. You'll be prepared for whatever the future holds in the finance industry if you put equal emphasis on honing your interpersonal and technical skills.

Conclusion: Your Finance Career Starts Now

We've concluded that a strong CV alone won't be enough to get you a job in the exciting and lucrative finance industry. The key is to comprehend the terrain develop your abilities constantly and forge relationships that will help you advance. The tactics we've covered are a guide for navigating a challenging industry where opportunities abound for those who are ready not just actions to take. Keep in mind that there are sometimes non-linear paths to your ideal finance position.

You may experience failures but every obstacle presents an opportunity for growth and learning. Accept internships intentionally network and develop your brand. These experiences will help you stand out in a crowded job market and improve your resume as well. The finance sector is always changing so it's important to remain flexible. Be aware of new trends and receptive to lifelong learning.

Your commitment to professional development will help you thrive and advance in your career. Have faith that you can make a difference as you begin this new chapter. The financial industry is looking for people with your kind of commitment new ideas and fresh perspectives. Your journey starts right now so confidently take that first step and know that success is just around the corner. Your ideal position in finance is not merely a pipe dream it's your destiny. Proceed with it!

www.ingramcontent.com/pod-product-compliance
Lightning Source LLC
Chambersburg PA
CBHW070413230526
45471CB00006B/2778